The Ultimate Injustice

by John Hlava

Published by the HFL Trust

Copyright 2015

Moreno Valley, California

INTRODUCTION

I write this not to offend, attack, or condemn any person or political party, but quite honestly to gently persuade individual thinking minds, and share other good people's thoughts and perspectives in an honest and open minded way, as to why many of us see induced abortion as something out of line with an evolved and 'civilized' civilization.

I simply ask you to read, to think about it, and then **get informed on your own** about the realities of induced abortion and the actual procedure, whether it's on the Internet, You Tube, or with your personal physician. **There are alternatives** to this injustice which many people are unaware of, and could possibly appease all parties involved, thus taking some of the hate and anger out of this highly contentious and controversial issue. Please open your mind to other perspectives and consider some of the potential alternative solutions which could benefit all parties involved. Thank you.

DEDICATION

I dedicate this short, but important and informative little booklet to God, who I frequently and repeatedly learned during my six decades gives us life, a soul, guides us, and tests us throughout our impetuous and sometimes reckless lives. He does this whether we choose to be 'believers' or not. He allows us to make our decisions, whether good or bad. He is the one who makes the real rules for life, and ultimately determines what is right and what is wrong. He has been overlooked a lot lately.

My other book 'Where's God These Days?' shares numerous personal experiences which have 'proven' to me that He really is still here, always guiding us, yet giving us the 'free will' to make our own choices for better or for worse. Unfortunately, my first hand experiences, or 'proof' of God's existence cannot be passed along to any individual. 'Proof' cannot be transmitted from one person to another. Mere words are the closest we can come to sharing that learned 'proof' with each other.

Table of Contents

Injustice: It's All Too Common in our World

We all experience injustice. It is inevitable on Earth. Yes, some have endured more than others. Some of us are blessed, and some of us have suffered in our lifetimes; but most of us have experienced both blessings and suffering. We have all experienced injustice to one degree or another. It is part of our background no matter who we have evolved from.

I am from a European background. European populations have been overrun many times by barbaric armies that slaughtered and tortured those whom they've conquered. As recently as the 20th century, less than 100 years ago, millions of my ancestors, were tortured, and used for genetic experimentation, and literally slaughtered like cattle by other cultures who thought a little bit differently, and felt they were superior, and thought they had a better way to run the world. In the last century, genocide was actually quite commonplace among Black, White, Asian, European, and Native American cultures among many others.

Hutus massacred up to one million Tutsis by hacking them to death with machetes. We all know the injustices that African Americans have suffered for centuries, even here in the most evolved and advanced nation on the planet, the United States. Many souls still suffer horrific torture and injustices around the world on a daily basis.

Even today in the 21st century, slavery persists in the world. Many still suffer. The slavery may be compensated for by a few coins, a favor, a little rice or a bit of grain, but many in the primitive lands are surviving on almost nothing. We must teach them how to fix these inequities, but we certainly must not replicate the systems that created those positions.

However, if we look back a few centuries at human history, we can be pleased to learn that the world is very slowly changing and beginning to become a more compassionate place for us common citizens. However, there remain some issues that we still need to work on.

Every living thing, every plant, every animal has to compete for a place to exist on this planet. We live in a finite world with limited resources. There are often shortages in the material things we need in order to survive. We sometimes have to fight for what we need to stay alive. This competition often creates disharmony. But we should never deprive any human life at its very beginning from the 'right' to be born and subsequently live. All living things deserve an opportunity, a place here, a chance to live, and a chance to fight to survive.

I personally have always favored the underdog, the overlooked, the more challenged in the competition. I have supported those who were not able to defend themselves, or even speak for themselves. I have always felt as the age old adage says, "God helps those who help themselves." I admire those who strive hard for their share. Once we reach the age of adulthood and have the ability to think and reason for ourselves, we have the ability to help ourselves, defend ourselves, and improve ourselves. However, infants and young children usually cannot express their thoughts and opinions, yet they have many of the universal human 'rights' which are often overlooked by people for some strange reason.

I recognize the many injustices that yet exist in the world. THERE ARE TOO MANY!! However, I consider this particular injustice to the youngest members of the human race to be "the ultimate injustice" because of its commonality, sheer brutality, and its disregard for the most helpless of all human beings.

Unlike other victims of injustice, these victims are 'developed' and 'developing' babies, and so they have no voice with which to object to what is being done to them. It is being done hundreds of times a day, and the method which is used to end their life is nothing short of unconscionable brutality. Look into it.

Check it out for yourself. I have tried to observe the actual abortion procedure many times, but I often had to look away because it is what I consider "too sick to watch." If one wishes to have a valid, intelligent opinion on this volatile subject, they need to view these realities and become informed.

Another characteristic of the common injustices that we have in the world is unfamiliarity with those who are the true victims. This unfamiliarity translates into ignorance about the subject. It's easy to be cruel and brutal if we know nothing about the victims. We find it easy to curse or hate those we do not know personally. But with those whom we've met and learned from, and shared a piece of our life with, it is much more difficult to be cruel and brutal.

It is much easier to tell the doctor to kill the young embryo, than it is to think of killing our two year old child who was once that embryo.

14

When Life Starts And Its Point of Independence

No thinking person disputes the fact of when 'life' starts in the womb. Life exists in the womb even before an egg is fertilized. It's a total living environment in itself, even before any conception. The living womb has the incredible, seemingly impossible potential to reproduce a living copy from the two human donors who have contributed a microscopic part of themselves.

Most of us learned in junior high biology that once a sperm meets an egg, a new unique life automatically begins its metamorphosis, growth, and development. It doesn't happen overnight where it's a young life as an embryo one day, and the next day it's a developed viable human being, capable of living on its own.   It happens in small stages, minute by minute and day by day until it achieves independence, the ability to live on its own, while still remaining inside the womb.

For many weeks after conception, the fertilized egg grows, getting closer to resembling the human beings that have contributed the sperm and the egg.   It has been argued that the newly fertilized egg in its first few weeks is nothing more than an appendage of the mother.   But it truly is a new life.   It is a bit of the father, and a bit of the mother.   Yes, in the beginning it is dependent on the mother, yet separate and unique because it also has elements of the father. This is not a clear cut, black and white issue.   It is a 'matter of degree' seeing there are dramatic changes going on with that new entity every hour of every day.   Furthermore, only God knows when the 'soul' enters this new body.   But we do know that the nervous system with its ability to feel pain is forming in the very first trimester, and this nervous system has developed extensively by the second trimester.

Whenever this life starts in a mother these days, it is sometimes taken very lightly as an inconvenient condition of the mother. However, this young life, whether it's in its first week or its 39th week, is a real human life with a possible future life expectancy of 90 or even 100 years if it is left to live.   Imagine what might be accomplished in that long life. History of the world has often been changed by one individual.

Today's medical and scientific advancements are making it a common possibility for a young baby today to live well into the 22nd century. Looking at this realistic 'big picture' should give us a different perspective on that young life, whether it is a one week old embryo or a fully developed human being in its third trimester, just waiting for the formality of passing through the birth canal.

At this point it is capable of living without its host mother while it is still inside the mother.

It is a viable human being, complete with all its bodily functions.   It has nerves to feel, ears to hear, and eyes to see its hand in front of its face.

It is also capable of hearing an approaching forceps and feeling its pressure on its bodily parts that may be caused by a doctor's intention to abort the pregnancy, because it is the mother's 'right to choose' even at the last minute, if she claims it would be a hardship to have the child.

A Mother's "Right to Choose"

It is an indisputable fact that most mothers and fathers think of the death of their young child as the most horrific experience a person could go through in life; worse than the death of a parent and worse than the death of a spouse. But not all mothers and fathers think this way. These opinions vary based on the background and life experience of those individuals. It doesn't mean that some mothers are bad and some are good. It just means that their background is influencing their judgment one way or the other. When it comes to induced abortion, it could also be a matter of which mothers are informed about the procedure and the consequences, and which are not.

The term "a mother's right to choose" is very frequently used by those who condone the act of abortion.   I think we all totally agree with a mother's "rights."   My question is, "Didn't that right to choose also exist at the time of conception?"

Didn't that right also exist during the 13 weeks of the **first** trimester?"   If the mother got so far as the second trimester, didn't she already make a 'choice' to go that far?   Mothers like everyone else have a 'right' to choose about the issues in their life, but don't they also have responsibility?   A mother certainly has a 'right' to choose, but once a human life begins growing inside her, doesn't she also have the 'responsibility' to consider a father's thoughts or the child's feelings on what will become a matter of human life and death?   Doesn't she have a 'responsibility' to chose 'wisely' sometime before the controversial second trimester and certainly before the 39th week?

This life didn't just suddenly pop into the mother's womb as a fully developed, easily recognizable, viable human infant, ready for the birthing stage of its existence.   This embryo grew from a tiny life smaller than a pea into a fully developed, easily recognized, independent human being inside the mother during the normal 39 week pregnancy. Why does that proclaimed "right to choose" only seem to exist in the second and third trimester? A choice was obviously made in the early weeks of pregnancy when the mother continued with the life. What many of us object to is a mother's right to 'change her mind,' after the life becomes an independent human which is no longer dependent on its host.

This baby has become a viable human being, and it could have existed totally independent of the mother, without the connecting umbilical cord, ever since its 22nd week. It's been proven. It's happened. But once it has evolved, through the 'choice' of the mother, to the stage of independence, it clearly should not be legal to kill it.

If a mother is too irresponsible to rectify her situation and exercise her "right to choose" during conception, or in the first few weeks of pregnancy, she should no longer have that "right to choose" in the second and third trimester after that baby has developed into a recognizable viable complete human being.

It also should be an issue of a "fathers right to choose" because he too had an important part in the creating of this young life.   If he is accepting of his responsibility, he too should have input into the future of the life he helped create.   Yes the mother is the one physically carrying the child.   However, the father often cares as much, or more than the mother about the young life that is equally a part of him.

Many thinking people who have investigated this procedure and its legalities wonder, "Why are we even discussing this?"   Why is this even an issue in a civilized evolved culture that has put a man on the moon, a robot on Mars, and created the magic of hand held computers. This same culture is continually chanting ridiculously about the "rights" of some of the most inane primitive creatures, and for the existence of some of the most foolish thoughtless causes.   Here is the start of a real person, a human being.   If left to develop according to nature, this child could live to fulfill 90 – 100 years of life. What may that person accomplish in their life? How could we kill them in the first few weeks of their natural existence?

Yes it is legal, deemed so by the U.S. Supreme Court. There have been so many Supreme Court decisions on this subject. Those decisions have gone back and forth. But ultimately, if it poses a hardship to the mother, it can be killed in the womb a day before it would be delivered naturally on its original due date!

Our Supreme Court has made many mistakes long before this issue came before them. This is not the first mistake for this all knowing 'justice seeking' entity, and unfortunately it will probably not be the last.

The Doctor's Actual Abortion Process

In this section, I encourage readers to do some simple, quick, and easy research on their own. There are so many sources of information available to us about any subject an individual is curious about. Please, don't just take my word or the word of any other individual as the 'end all.' Explore the Internet on your own. There is so much available beyond mere words regarding the actual process of induced abortion, which must be seen in order for a person to have an intelligent, informed opinion on this very controversial issue. To 'ignore' any actual events, opinions, or accepted facts on an important issue is 'ignorance' by its definition.

Almost everybody has an opinion on most issues these days. Unfortunately, half of these people are greatly uninformed about the facts involving these issues, or they have only listened to one side over and over without being receptive to any other opinion. It's proven that we've become so much more lazy, and apathetic as a society than we were a short 50 years ago, and it has taken its toll. Numerous private and government agencies have reported that our society has become seriously overweight, more apathetic, and far less informed about current issues that affect us, just in the last 20 years. But that doesn't stop us from chanting and screaming what we have to say, because it is our 'right' to do so.

For example, almost everybody has an opinion on abortion. But fewer than 16% of those people have looked up the subject, the legalities, the actual steps taken by a doctor to perform the procedure. The public spends millions of hours in front of their computers on-line every day. Yet few have invested three or four minutes to simply Google "the abortion process" in order to learn about this common practice. If we look around, we can see that the American public has indeed become more overweight, more apathetic, more lazy, and less informed about important issues.

This is dangerous, because as we fall into this pit, we lose the sense of good judgment, which determines pretty much everything in our lives.

Those of us who have been a resident of this planet for six or more decades, can clearly look back and see how our ability to relate with others, our quality of personal life, our security, and our attitudes have been adversely affected even as our technology has made major strides forward.   We pay more attention to drugs, Hollywood celebrities, and superficial subject matter, than we do to who has the qualifications to lead us, or true and authentic injustice where it exists in the world.   We need to relearn what is important to learn.

The Christian Perspective and the Bible

Every knowledgeable Christian understands that the one true God, the overseer of the universe is about life, love, good, truth, growth, improvement, nurturing, self actualization, and building up. This is the opposite of some prominent so-called 'religions' which produce hate, anger, destruction, killing, deceit and intolerance. If one looks at the Bible, they can clearly see the message. But so few people are paying attention anymore to what the Bible says. Does ending any life inside the womb of a host, simply because of the inconvenience, fit the teachings of the Bible?

All the major religions of the world have had their dark moments in world history; those horrific events and periods in time which they can be criticized for. However, most religions have evolved past the 12th century frame of mind.

Today in the 21st century, some self proclaimed Christians, some modern political parties, and the Supreme Court of our advanced nation actually condone the killing of a human infant in the womb by lethal injection, and then the removal of their body parts piece by piece with the use of a forceps. Occasionally, that living human creature is not injected with poison, but is simply dismembered piece by piece while it is still alive. It is all 'legal.' It is obviously not right, but it is legal.

As our population sheds our spiritual background and thinking in lieu of science driven materialism, we find a corresponding lack of compassion and tolerance which the Bible promotes. Good judgment also is becoming much more rare in our leaders and in our general population.

'Judgment' involves the ability to identify when 'murder' applies to situations in our society. The Bible has always helped guide us in the past with judgment calls. Judgment is needed in this issue when we consider the fact that a fully developed baby in the womb, who is ready for their natural full term birth, can legally be killed and dismembered, to remove it from the mother's womb if the mother can prove that having that child would be a hardship on her. For example, the baby could have an identified due date of December 25th all through the natural pregnancy, as was the case with our son. On December 24th it is legal to give that baby a lethal injection to kill it and then remove him piece by piece from the uterus with a forceps. If that same child is born on the 25th, suddenly a parent will go to prison for murder if they kill that child one or two days later than when it was 'legal.' The only difference is that it passed through the birth canal. It wasn't any less of a developed human being one or two days before.

This scenario of a 'legal' end of term abortion happens all the time, just as new parents with a newborn baby murdering the newborn has happened too often.

It is 'legal' to kill the child one day, but a 'crime' leading to a prison term the next day. Does this reality make any sense?

This should clearly demonstrate how out of line the common practice of viable abortion is with a civilized society. It also demonstrates how judgment is lacking today, even among our political leaders and our Supreme Court.

Citizens of the world need to think for themselves, with the frequency that people used to, and not lazily look for someone else to do their thinking for them and relying on a political party or others to legislate what is 'right and wrong.'

The Bible has a useful purpose for us as today, as much or more than it did 50 years ago. Christians as well as other 'thinking' people need to look closer at the realities of this "ultimate injustice."

So Much Hypocrisy

Today we often see people demonstrating that it is all about them, and they are the ONLY ones that matter. Our population often feels THEY are the only one with rights, while totally overlooking everyone else's rights. They often deny personal responsibility, or pass the blame along, yet demand their rights with great enthusiasm. And we are acquiring so much compassion for wild animals, which is a good thing, yet we kill hundreds of babies every day here in the U.S. simply because it is "a mother's right to choose." We disregard the fact that the baby is an aware human being, with its own heart that begins beating in week 3, with nerves that feel pain and pleasure. And later that baby is fully developed and capable of living on its own without any more help from the mother. It has become a unique individual human, about to become a little girl or little boy.

Our hypocritical public demonstrates in the streets and seems to care more about a lion shot in the wild of Africa, or chickens being too crowded in a cage, or a pampered killer whale being unhappy in captivity, than they do about the life or death of a human baby.

When child molesters and child killers go to prison, they are usually targeted for punishment for their crimes by the general population in that prison. This is because even those convicted criminals, who we think of as the worst of our civilization, have more compassion for the innocent and defenseless little people, than many of the citizens freely walking the streets every day. Many of those criminals who are often called "the most brutal of our society" consider abortion as an abomination because of its brutality. Many of the free citizens on the street claim to be compassionate and responsible. Sometimes they are, but very selectively, and many of those free thinking citizens call themselves Christians.

Healthy, clear thinking, well adjusted individuals treasure life. They may take someone's life if someone threatens to brutally take away theirs, or other innocent lives. This is understandable. But life is treasured by most people and should be sustained. We seem to treasure 'nature' but yet we allow many to cut it short when it consists of a new life in a womb.

There is so much hypocrisy that exists with people who claim to be understanding, yet they refuse to see any other point of view. They may refuse to deviate from the comfort of their political party's platform, or even listen to other points of view. If one listens to an opposing point of view, and then chooses to reject it, that is understandable. But that requires thinking. Today, with our lazy, uninformed culture, we can see many who don't even listen to the other sides of a multi faceted issue. They prefer to listen only to those who agree with them because it's so much easier than trying to look at an issue from a different perspective.

We march in the streets and have protests to free the killer whales at ocean aquariums, because we imagine they are unhappy. We throw paint on women and their fur coats to protest the use of a dead animal's fur. We push for the closing of zoos, because they cage wild animals and we assume the animals are poorly cared for. We oppose the use of any animals, even rats, in researching drugs or medicines that could potentially save human lives. We have social uproar over the killing of an animal in the wild, a lion that was shot legally by a hunter in Africa, despite the fact that the lion was a regular killer of other animals. The hunter who was hunting legally even received death threats.

If a mother and father produce a new life in the womb and allow it to develop, it is their responsibility to care for that life, because that child is not an animal in the wild, but a living human being with a heart that's beating, nerves that can feel, and a brain that has developed.

Life should not be taken away simply because it is deemed inconvenient or a financial burden. The decisions we make in our youth can lead to regrets for the rest of our lives. Many mature adults have later regretted the decision to give up a baby during the stressful time of an unplanned pregnancy. The consequences of our actions seem to inevitably catch up with us, whether it is criminal behavior or just poor judgment during a challenging period in our lives. Fortunately thinking people are able to improve with time, and see their own faults from their younger years. We must pass on what we have learned.

Responsibility and Compassion

"It's not all about me!" When was the last time you heard someone say that? "I really need to be more responsible!" These are expressions which are not heard at all. Quite the opposite.

No civilized society can exist without responsibility and compassion. They demonstrate a willingness to accept a positive, contributing role in a life among other people, and to care about those other souls. It is not a selfish, negative 'take all I can' role that exploits the society. Without responsibility and compassion, a society is just a mass of individuals with no ties or relationships with anyone else. It's a mob made up of untrustworthy individuals who are out for themselves Responsibility is related to self discipline. Self discipline is the acceptance of responsibility for ourselves, to ourselves. And there is an abundance of evidence in the news everyday that self discipline is waning as much as personal responsibility and compassion all around the world.

We all make mistakes. We all demonstrate poor judgment at times, especially when we are very young and do not have the repertoire of life experiences to draw from. Our leaders also make many mistakes, and those are often in the spotlight. But it is rare to find one of those leaders who will admit to being wrong. Even they often fail to take responsibility for their lack of good judgment and their bad behavior. Many of them will blatantly lie to the world before taking responsibility. This trait is not exclusive to any one political party. They often lack compassion as well, using their positions to exploit people and situations.

Unfortunately, the result is that the world sees this behavior from its 'leaders' and it becomes commonplace within the society.

However, the major cause of this lack of responsibility and compassion in society is in the homes.   These virtues are not taught enough by responsible parents.   Children learn behavior too often on the streets and on the unsupervised playgrounds.   Then they come home from school and become hypnotically transfixed on video games which develop their skills in killing an adversary who is out to get them.   Movies put out by the Hollywood moneymakers only add to this unfortunate situation.   The result is a lack of compassion, in lieu of 'get them before they get me.'

These children grow up to become parents, and leaders of society who see personal convenience as more important than life itself. If a baby must die to preserve a convenient lifestyle, so be it.

A Baby's Rights After the Birth

Yes, mothers have rights. Fathers have rights. Children have rights. Even babies have rights. But babies are the only one of these groups that cannot demand or even express their rights. Yes they can cry when they are hungry, or when they are in discomfort; but they cannot express much more than this. When they do cry, they are communicating to the best of their ability. This is when the mother's and father's 'responsibility' kicks in to feed the baby, change the baby, hold and bond with the baby, or try to find a solution to that discomfort. Those are a baby' rights!!

Their first and most important right is to live a life that started about nine months earlier. As they continue to grow outside the womb, they will acquire more rights until they reach adulthood, when they will have many rights, like driving a car, becoming educated, having their own children, and the right to pursue happiness.

In fact, the most important and influential years in that baby's life is the first 5 years, because what this person sees, feels and experiences in these early years sets the foundation for that person's personality and attitude. That personality and attitude will guide them throughout their life and will influence every decision they make, good or bad.

As a career educator and teacher for many years in elementary schools, I have clearly seen the difference between the children who were nurtured and had a lot of interaction with others in those early years, and those that spent more time alone, without interaction and stimulation. Even more sad is when we see the evidence that a child was neglected, abused, or affected in the womb by alcohol or drugs. It becomes so obvious very quickly in their life that they have this burden placed on them because of the lack of diligence in their upbringing.

Because of the fact that mothers and fathers are capable of expressing their own rights, and taking care of themselves, I feel the 'rights' of the unborn and newly born people should actually have priority in our society.   The weak, the small, and the challenged members of our culture need a little extra care, to be looked after, and monitored by our civilization as a whole, if we want to really be compassionate and fair with 'every ones rights.'

Evolution of Our Primitive 'Civilization'

We are continually evolving as a world society, gaining knowledge, wisdom, compassion and insight.   If we looked back into our past, we would see so much brutality and cruelty because it was much more commonplace back in the distant past.   We have come a long way, but we only need to read the news to see that we still have a long way to go.   But at least we are talking about these issues constantly today.

In our culture here in the U.S., we are obsessed with being "politically correct."   We boycott eggs that were not laid by free range chickens who were allowed to happily roam and frolic. We become "offended" by some of the slightest, most absurd and insignificant actions of others.   So why do we intentionally kill human babies who are fully developed and capable of living without the mother, but simply have not yet passed through a woman's birth canal?   Our culture is slowly making progress and becoming more civilized and compassionate, even though our priorities are still screwed up.

When a child begins to grow in a woman's womb, that child is a 'blank slate.'   If allowed to live, they will develop throughout their life, they will inevitably learn many new things. They will love as we all have loved, and be thought of as a 'pure blessing' to someone they meet.   They may develop into a blessing for the entire world, because we teach our children, "With hard work and a good heart, they can become anything they wish to be." That child could grow to become another Nelson Mandela, John F. Kennedy, Mother Teresa, Albert Einstein, a pope, or a heroic world leader.

I think about the human race 100 years from now.   I imagine the advances in science and technology.   I try to picture what it would be like to live in that time.   Humans who have not been aborted but have been allowed to pass through a woman's birth canal will probably be living well past the age of 100 years old. I also think we will be looking back on this controversial issue of abortion today much the same way we look back today on the common barbarism and brutality of the 1600's. I think we will question our past judgment, and be asking ourselves, "How could we have allowed that to happen?"

Of all the conflicts yet to be resolved in the future, I think abortion is one of those areas of conflict which we will look back upon and recognize for its 'brutality, and lack of compassion and understanding. I hope that one day in the future, when humanity becomes more evolved, refined and civilized, we will look back to these days as a misguided period in our development, much as a young mother may look back on her choice to abort a child when she was young, uninformed, and misguided.

Exceptions and Alternatives

I do believe there should be exceptions on this very controversial issue. Killing a human is never good; never. But unfortunately there are times when abortion is simply 'the least of all evils.' We have to look at situations of rape and whether or not it applies or is being exploited. That needs to be determined. In cases where there is severe natural damage to the embryo, disease, or serious injury, it needs to be decided if a life of suffering is best for a child and family, or if early stage abortion should be considered. These exceptions need to examined and judged on an individual basis.

In no way should a difficult pregnancy threaten the life of a mother through complications. If it becomes a decision to save a baby or save a mother, the 'lesser of the two evils' dictates we should save the mother. It's only common sense.

With today's technology and medical advances, we are able to detect when and if a pregnancy is prone to complications. We are able to look at a pregnancy in its early stages, and often predict the outcome, and monitor its development and progress every day.

If the mother has made her 'choice' to allow the pregnancy to progress to an advanced stage, and then makes the decision that she does not want the baby, many alternatives exist.

'Safe Surrender' in many states allows for a mother to take an unwanted baby to a hospital or fire station, and give up that baby into a safe, caring environment that will continue to watch over that child and find an eventual home.

There are also many married couples unable to conceive a child who would treasure the opportunity to raise an adopted baby in a loving, nurturing home.

It has often occurred that a young mother and father who feel incapable of raising a child would surrender the young child to a family member or acquaintance who is willing to raise that child and share them throughout their life with the natural mother and father. This often enables the natural parents to maintain some relationship with their child.

Many agencies exist throughout the U.S. to aid a mother in finding a workable and compassionate solution to a 'problem' free of charge.

And then, there are 'choices' that a woman and man should be free to make. Specifically, those choices are to use a condom, a calendar to determine the safe time of the month, a pill, or simple old fashioned abstinence.

But very often we read in the newspaper or hear on the news how a newborn baby has been dumped in a dumpster or just left out in the cold. This lack of judgment, lack of compassion, and lack of common sense is not unusual for a teenager going through the stress of an unwanted pregnancy.

All of us have been young and have done many stupid things. It's unfortunate and very wrong when a civilized society and its leaders condone this ultimate injustice of abortion.

We have an inherent responsibility to preserve and nurture life. We need to strive to attain our ability for individual thinking, accepting our responsibilities, and demonstrating compassion. It is our most potent birthright as well as our duty. We must not relinquish these virtues.

When there is so much knowledge at our fingertips on the Internet and elsewhere, we have a responsibility to become informed about our world, and not give in to the tendency to ignore what we do not want to know, simply because it makes us uncomfortable. The root word of 'ignorance' is the word 'ignore.'

Let's make the effort to learn the full reality of issues that affect us and our world. This responsibility is not limited to abortion, but abortion does remain one of the most critical issues of life and death in our world, and it will affect our future if we continue to kill our future fellow citizens.

Things to Think About

What's love?   Love has babies,   sex has abortions.

-Fey Weldon-

The 'right to life' is the first among human rights.

-Pope Francis

A woman has a 'right to choose.'   But the time to choose is before, not after it's too late.

-J Wadsworth Hart-

It clearly seems to me that abortion would be a crime.

-Gandhi-

A person is a person, no matter how small.

-Dr Seuss-

The littlest feet make the biggest footprints in our hearts and lives.

-unknown-

Life is a test.   It tests our judgment and attitudes toward life, then rewards us accordingly.

-J Wadsworth Hart-

People often say abortion is a woman's choice, and they're right.   They choose life the moment they have sex.

-Preston Wagner-

Abortion is a weapon of mass destruction against the voiceless.

-E A Bucchianeri-

It is a crime to decide that a child must die so that you may live as you wish.

-Mother Teresa-

It seems to me that women who say, "It is my body and my choice" are overlooking the other human body inside them.

-J Wadsworth Hart-

The littlest person can change the course of the future.

-J R R Tolkien-

I've noticed that everyone who is in favor of abortion has already been born.

-Ronald Reagan-

Abortion is murder of the innocent before they've had a chance to express their opinion.

unknown

When listening to one argue in favor of abortion, we can often see the one who should have been aborted.

-J Wadsworth Hart-

I certainly support the woman's right to choose, but in my mind, the time to choose is before, not after the fact.

Ann Ross

www.ingramcontent.com/pod-product-compliance
Lightning Source LLC
Chambersburg PA
CBHW071240280526
45788CB00004B/1520